A) Are you a carbon-based life form!

B) Do you walk erect on two legs (most of the time)?

C) Do you have $7.99?

If you answered yes to question C, then you're our kind of gal! You are the person our sophisticated, 21st-century market research has identified as our most likely victim, er, reader.

So buy this book and start breaking the rules. We'll teach you how to :

- Be needy, clingy and whiny with Mr. Right Now.
- Ransom his power tools to get his attention.
- Repair used blenders for fun and profit.

And we'll make money! Isn't capitalism great? Is there anything else we can sell you? Have we told you about our $100-per-minute seminars? Wanna buy a T-shirt?

BREAKING
THE
R·U·L·E·S

Last-ditch tactics for landing the man of your dreams

By Laura Banks & Janette Barber

CAREER PRESS
3 Tice Road
P.O. Box 687
Franklin Lakes, NJ 07417
1-800-CAREER-1
201-848-0310 (NJ and outside U.S.)
FAX: 201-848-1727

BREAKING THE RULES
ISBN 1-56414-296-5, $7.99
Cover design by Tom Phon
Printed in the U.S.A. by Book-mart Press

To order this title by mail, please include price as noted above, $2.50 handling per order, and $1.00 for each book ordered. Send to: Career Press, Inc., 3 Tice Road, P.O. Box 687, Franklin Lakes, NJ 07417.

Or call toll-free 1-800-CAREER-1 (NJ and Canada: 201-848-0310) to order using VISA or MasterCard, or for further information on books from Career Press.

Dedication

Janette: To Barry Brown.

Laura: To myself, for putting up with me all these years.

Acknowledgments

There are a number of people we would like to thank (ow), but, er, our publisher, Ron Fry, has suggested (hey, that hurts!), in the *nicest* possible way, that we talk about him and how important he was to this entire project. Which we certainly would have done in any case because he is really ~~great nice wonderful~~ an incredible stud puppet who makes us quiver like jellyfish with his masculine, muscular body and his enormous ~~ego feet~~ (OW. Now that *really* hurt.)

So anyway, Ron is just the best publisher two women could ever want. Did we mention his muscles? Quivering? Like jellyfish? Enormous? Right.

We are just so pleased that we had the good fortune to have Ron. Without him, this book would not have been so ~~trashy poorly edited embarrassing~~ scintillating, so enormous, so muscular, oh, never mind.

Laura and Janette

Please! He made us write this! Buy the book! Save us!

Contents

All rules are made to be broken

We think it's weird. As liberated as women like to think they've become, many of our girlfriends are still sitting around waiting for a man to sweep them off their feet, marry them and solve all their problems.

This desperate man-catching must have started at some point in the distant past, when a wounded cavewoman too weak to hunt for herself had to depend on a caveman to bring her mastodon meat so she wouldn't starve. Ever since, human females have been teaching their girl-child offspring to follow an archaic set of rules designed to entrap men into marriage (this is where the freezer gets filled and we see the mastodon meat connection). Well, *we* don't want to merely survive. We want to live!

So that's what we've done. Sometimes we're in relationships, sometimes we're not, but we're always having a good time doing it. Let's face it, we're young (enough), prettier than Olive Oyl, successful and fun to be with (we have references on this one). We don't follow rules—we break them.

And we invite you to break them with us!

WARNING:

This is not your
grandmother's book
of dating tips!

1

Force yourself on men and tell them what they're thinking

"Do you come here often?"

"Care to share a double-double-decaf-decaf-Amaretto-latte?"

"What's your Social Security number and mother's maiden name?"

Any opening will do. Be tough, be strong, be aggressive. Anyplace. Anytime. If you don't quickly come on to that hunk across the room at Starbucks, there's a good chance you'll never meet him. Men never say hello to strange women! None of our friends ever get approached by men in public, except, of course, by guys with names that are either all consonants or all vowels, who are: a) desperate for their next cab fare, or b) seeking someone to sponsor them for their green card.

You have to stare a man down, make him whimper, make him cower. Get right in his face and lick his cheek. Remember, most men suffer from xenophobia—they're scared of strangers. And that means *you*, at least until you fall into his lap. Otherwise, he'd rather be home playing with his power tools than actually stutter something, *any*thing, to a real live woman.

Yes, you can do your best Scarlett O'Hara ("Why Ashley Wilkes, I never..." flutter flutter titter titter) and look away, pretending to be coy and weak and nonthreatening. Then you can watch the in-your-face babe stroll out trailed by a conga line of drooling hunks. To get him to look beyond his own nose, you must convince him from the beginning that you're fun, easy(going) and his for the asking. You must come on assertively. Don't pretend for a minute that you're not going to lead him around by his nose, though we recommend waiting until the *second* date to actually *fit* him for the nose ring, with or without the optional leash. By talking to the man first or asking him to dance, he'll have no illusion about who's in charge, and who's going to *stay* in charge.

You're probably thinking this seems a bit severe, not to mention pushy and overbearing. Pshaw! *Real* torture is listening to William Shatner sing "Lucy in the Sky With Diamonds" (we are not making this up—we have the record). Breaking the Rules (BTR) women don't give a damn! Speaking first to Mr. Cappuccino doesn't give him a chance to talk to another woman he might find more attractive. Whatever the cost, even if you have to sit on his hands, be the first woman to get his attention. Stare at him and all his neediness will coming pouring out. Then you can get him to do anything you want.

Remember, dating is like a game of bridge. You either wind up sitting across from a dummy or trying for a slam, unless, of course, you're sitting east-northeast at even vulnerability with a hangover, in which case you club your partner with your diamond and break his heart.

Men are not the macho tigers they pretend to see in the mirror every morning. They are actually shy, insecure insects with no guts. They're stuck in emotional cocoons, living on fantasies, unable to muster the courage to do more than sneak a peek at you when they think you're not looking. (We checked with a few of our guy friends. They all backed us up on this. And they all made us promise not to use their names.)

Face it, ladies, we've confused these incredible hulks to no end. Just when they thought macho was in, we threw Tom Hanks at them—a guy who cries at the *Oscars*, for gosh sakes—and simpered about how wonderful he was because he just lived and breathed *to please his wife*. We demanded that they *talk about their feelings*, which *really* lead to confusion. Now we have to put up with men *pretending* to have feelings when they are still the same gutless oafs they were before: "Okay, I'm really in touch with my inner child," they simper, "*now* can we get naked?"

That's why BTR women have to get to the point. Show him who's boss by always going dutch or paying for everything. Get over it. You are a woman of the 90s. This guy probably earns less than you. And what he does earn goes to his first wife and three kids.

So always start the conversation. First, of course, make sure he's the guy for you. Does he have a pulse? Great, you're in business. Walk over to him, say hello and sit down at his table. Relax, laugh, make crude jokes, stare at him, lick your lips, give him your phone number. Drink as much as you want. It will loosen your tongue, among other things, and if he can stand you after watching you stagger around like a wino on Aqua Velva, you may have caught a live one!

Trick him into a business conversation, if need be, about how you've heard his firm is merging with yours. Suggest you go up to your place and review office positions. Offer to strip his long-term bond if he'll extend his option. He'll get the message. Men have no idea what they want until you ask for it.

What if you're interested in a man you really *do* work with? BTR methods still apply: Paste racy pictures of yourself in his cubicle (if necessary, cut his boss out of the pictures first). Send him e-mail that'll melt his hard drive. Suggest you dress in costume for your first date, as matching ice cream sundaes. Don't forget to specify who brings the whipped cream and chocolate sauce.

Call him all the time. This way, you don't have to go through the emotional hell of waiting for him to call you, presuming he ever gets up the courage to actually pick up the phone at all. If you wait, you'll dream up senseless, compulsive, obsessive fears trying to figure out his next move. You'll say things to yourself like, "Did he notice my perspiration stains? Should I have plucked my eyebrows before the date? Does he hate fat thighs? Were the hand-cuffs too tight?" Instead, call him. He'll come over. Then you'll be too busy to think about how fat your thighs actually are, even if they do chafe when you walk. It doesn't matter. He won't care. Men *despise* having to pick up the telephone and call a girl. It's leftover emotional baggage from high school. Trust us. He'll be *glad* you chased him down and demanded a relationship.

A close associate named Brenda met a man at a party and was thrilled with the results of talking to him first. It turned out he had been in a car accident and had *lost the ability to speak*. If Brenda hadn't said anything, he would have never been able to say hello! Six months later, they were married. It was a marriage based on equality because Brenda was free to be herself from the very beginning.

It was a great marriage while it lasted, but eventually he did leave her for his receptionist, Tammy Lynn Bambi Tiffany Loni Sue. Fortunately, this man was a terrific plastic surgeon and Brenda had gotten a face lift, a chin lift, a tummy tuck and a new nose. He was gone, but she happily found herself a new, younger husband who loved her youthful glow and hefty bank account. Let Brenda be a lesson to us all.

Unfortunately, there are still women out there who are afraid to break the rules and must suffer the consequences, no matter how dire. Another acquaintance, Mary, did *not* break the rules and lived to rue the day. Mary was at a party and, on the archaic advice of her grandmother, waited patiently to be asked to dance. She didn't look at any of the men in the room. She played demure, helpless and ridiculously feminine. She giggled. She sighed. After three days, seven hours and forty two minutes, Dick asked her to dance. She was thrilled. This was the traditional dating technique she had been told would work. And it had! So she continued doing all the sick things her grandmother had told her. She never revealed her thoughts, didn't return his phone calls and pretended to have no mind of her own. They married in three months.

Naturally, her marriage went downhill faster than a puppy strapped to a skateboard. Mary immediately discovered that they had nothing in common. She got more attention from her cat, Fluffy, who at least occasionally played with her socks. The moral of the story is: If you make him chase you, he will have captured his prey and never make another move again. Being courted and pursued by Dick, once he'd been merry with Mary, soon turned into, "Where's Dick?" And she never got any again.

Never let your life be like Mary's, without any Dick. Always ask a man to dance first. Here's how to seize the opportunity: The instant you spot your man across the room, rush to his side. Then, lightly brush your breasts against his arm. In that moment, he'll swoon and lose his balance. That's your chance. Grab him by the hair and drag him onto the floor. When he can't dance any more, drag him home.

Of course, there is one rule that must be followed without deviation: Never dance with a man who can't stand up, even if he asks you first. Our friend Anne learned the hard way. Trying to do things "the right way," she was ecstatic after seven hours of crocheting when Jimmy lurched over and asked her to dance. Ignoring the drool (on his lips) and dinner stains (on his lips) and large warts (on his lips), she was happy just to stagger around the dance floor, steering for the occasional wall so he could prop himself up between songs. Well, to make a short story overbearingly long, they wound up marrying and he wound up sobering up. And the moment he did, four years later, she was left standing in the foyer, with only a bottle of Ripple to remember him by.

A lesson for us all.

2

Stare straight at men and talk incessantly

Being unafraid of eye contact—early, steady, steely and often—is a sure sign of power and dominance, both qualities greatly admired by BTR women. How else is the poor baby across the room going to know that you're interested? Reading subtle signs is not the forte of the male species. Neither is asking for directions, making a decent salad dressing, or cleaning the hairs out of the sink, but we digress.

Maybe he *did* notice you and has been hoping you'd come on to him. Maybe he's a sweet, submissive man who can be induced to clean your apartment wearing nothing but a French maid's apron. Don't pass up what could be a good thing by avoiding the eye contact that will let you know if you have a chance.

Making blatant eye contact is a skill that can't be practiced enough. Do it with everyone. Stare them down. Make them quiver. Practice whenever you can—in the waiting room at the dentist, in line at the bank, on your best friend's husband. Don't even blink. Make them feel as if you are looking clear through them.

If you are, unaccountably, alone at a function, stare hungrily around for an unattached male. Loosen a top button. Bite your lip, smudge your makeup, look easy. If you can't have a good man, grab a handy man.

Daphne breaks the rules. She's tall, she's gorgeous, she's powerful. And she had a wonderful date last week with a man she met on the subway. He was gorgeous and she was interested, so she stared him right in the eye and smiled. He was a little taken aback. He wasn't used to a woman so bold, so beautiful, so incredibly self-assured, let alone one who used saran wrap as such a refreshing fashion accessory. He felt a stirring in his body, one that was somewhat inconvenient on the subway, in public, wearing pleated Armani pants.

He knew from the look on Daphne's face that she knew exactly what she was doing to him. She waited until the subway neared her stop. Then she stood up, the long folds of a silk dress gently caressing her body, her milky white thighs swishing, swishing to the rhythm of the train's hot, churning wheels as it entered the long, dark, yearning tunnel, and walked slowly across the not-too-crowded car. She stopped in front of him and smiled. "Hi," she purred.

"Want me to call you?"

This week we can't get in touch with her—they flew to Paris for the weekend.

Whatever you do, make yourself memorable. Experiment. Walk with a limp. Explore the question: *Do men spend more money on lame girls?*

On a first date, should you ever get that far, pretend he's Prince Charming and you're Snow White. Stare lovingly into his eyes at all times. Your imagination is all you need to turn that worthless sack of potatoes into a hot cross bun.

Make him think you are in love with him just to see what he'll do. Ignore your food and everyone and everything in the restaurant, even if something catches on fire. Make him feel like a fly struggling in your web as you get closer and closer to sucking him dry. He will feel strong and important if you give him this much attention. He will also be more likely to order the most expensive bottle of wine on the menu.

Treat every date as a free therapy session. It's your chance to thoroughly review your past with an eager listener who's hoping only to get laid. It's amazing what he'll put up with—and for how long—if he has the faintest hope of just *seeing* your bra sometime before the next full moon. Blather about your mother until he hates her, too, then nag and wheedle him into spending the weekend with her. Without *you*, of course—why would you want to spend a weekend with your mother?

Feel free to let him in on your opinions about the male orgasm and how just once you'd like a guy to last as long as Leno's monologue. Okay, Letterman's Top Ten List. Okay, Chevy Chase's stint as a talk-show host.

Light his fire with controversy. If he's a liberal, lecture him about the deep meaning of Rush Limbaugh's writings. Do your William F. Buckley imitation...over and over and over. If he's a conservative, arrange for your second date to start at a soup kitchen. Tell him you're Bella Abzug's cousin. Remind him every five minutes or so that you once saw JFK Jr. in Central Park. Whatever he likes, practice your sense of power by making him talk about the opposite.

Indulge in racy stories from your dating past. If necessary, make them up. Tell him about that one-night stand with the Iraqi who ran screaming from the bedroom when he discovered you *liked* sex. Tell him about that wonderful weekend with the crew of that British frigate who all had such adorable accents, not to mention that wonderful game they called Raising the Sails. Scare him with the story of how you handcuffed the illegal alien you'd been dating and rifled his apartment for the money he owed you after you discovered he was seeing another woman. Show him your Lorena Bobbitt Paring Knife, which works all right on carrots but... Don't hold back. Let him know what he's getting into.

Let him know you've a mind to be reckoned with, a brain with far more important things to do than memorize baseball lineups from 1942 and the measurements of the last 18 Miss Teen USAs. Quote articles from the latest issues of *Cellular Microbiology* and obscure Czech literary essays. Liberally sprinkle the nightstand with books like *Advanced Principles of Catalytic Converters, Quantum Physics for Incredibly Bright Women* and three different translations of *Finnegan's Wake*—Sanskrit, Bengali and Bulgarian. Remark casually about your recent correspondence with Stephen Hawking and how you just *must* dash off some e-mail so he can finish that new book. If you're smarter than he is, you might as well rub his eyeballs in it.

If you find yourself at one of those awkward moments where no one has anything to say, we suggest you read aloud. *One Hundred and Twenty Days of Sodom* by the Marquis de Sade is always a safe selection.

Men fall in love with you because they are afraid *not* to, so be careful to always keep them off balance with your incessant flow of meaningless conversation. We know one woman who talked so much that every man she went out with took her to bed just to get her to shut her mouth.

Update him constantly and consistently on how you think the date is going. A rating chart comes in handy, especially if it includes the names of his friends. Let him know you are a neurotic mess who might stalk him if you don't get your way. A playful jab with a fork in the fleshy part of his thigh will get the point across.

3

Meet him anywhere and tell him where to go

Dating is simply not a man's passion, so you've got to make it easy for him. When you decide you want to go out with him, always say something like, "Since I'm going to be driving right by your house, I'll pick you up in an hour. Don't make me wait." Pick the restaurant and make the reservation. Don't allow him to do any of the thinking or planning. He'd never *think* of picking up *Zagat's* and checking out reviews of local eateries. You're lucky if he remembers to put his pants on before the date. Can you imagine a guy calling a friend for information on a place to take you? That's about as likely to happen as him *asking for directions*. Oh, that's another good reason to meet him more than halfway—he won't get lost.

The truth is, men need to be told where to go. We all know that. Left alone in the kitchen, a man will take out an eye. The same holds true in dating. If you don't take the lead and make yourself extremely easy to catch and figure out, the man will never find his way out of his house. Remember, men will not work hard to see you. They're too busy thinking about the important things: beer, pretzels and lube jobs.

We made sissies out of men a long time ago, and now we have to live with it. Men will never rearrange their schedule to see you, chase you or find you. They're too busy being with the women who make themselves readily available. Witness the story of Danny, who drove from San Diego to Santa Barbara to see his gal. He ran out of gas halfway there and just left the car. Took a bus back home and called the girl around the corner who had been hanging around outside his apartment for weeks. She was dying to see him, and he knew exactly where she could be found. That's a successful BTR babe. (It's also a nonsensical story, lacking a traditional beginning, middle and end and any transitional elements, but who's quibbling?—Ed.)

It's important for Breaking the Rules women to go out of their way to meet men. Sit in his office with your feet on his desk and your skirt slightly raised…over your head. Paste an "I'm available" Post-It on your forehead. Did we mention that police lineups are much better than bars? These men are depressed, they're tired, they're handcuffed and they're yours for the asking (if you have $500 bail).

Another time-tested plan is to break into your favorite fellow's car and sit in the front seat until he comes out. Then surprise him with your best impression of Glenn Close in *Fatal Attraction* and scream, "Why didn't you call? Do you know how many pills I've already swallowed?" Before he collapses from an aneurism, burst out laughing and cover him with kisses. He'll be so glad you weren't for real, he'll let you drive him anywhere. Head for the hospital first so you can have the pills pumped out of your stomach.

Man catching, if done correctly, is a fabulous sport. If you break the rules you can be assured that any man you meet will treat you as the mysterious equal that you are. Why? Because he'll never know what you'll do next. Or what happened to his credit cards.

A good rule of thumb to remember is that men who drive many miles out of their way to see you are usually, at best, desperate and lonely people or, at worst, desperate and lonely people out on parole from the local penitentiary. Don't be surprised if he shows up with an ink tattoo on his forehead asking you for cigarettes and pocket change. If you accept a date with this man because his behind looks good in the orange jumpsuit, just make sure you're prepared to pay for dinner. License-plate making just doesn't pay as well as it used to.

If you're broke, take him to tacky hamburger joints in dangerous neighborhoods. If you make it home alive, the thrill of surviving the evening should set both your hearts aflutter. Order in cheap and greasy Chinese food. Feed him one mouthful at a time, sitting cross-legged on the floor wearing nothing but his boxer shorts. Slather him with soy sauce and play Find the Fortune Cookie.

Whatever you do, stop waiting for some nonexistent guy to come along and save you. Get over it. This is it. Get a job and buy your own stuff. And stop worrying about finding that "one" right guy. There are millions of them out there. The dating pool is like Price Club, where you don't buy a box of Cheerios, you buy a hogshead, Hawaiian Punch is available in shipping-tank size and mayonnaise is either a spread or a wrestling aid.

4

Carry an answering machine in your purse

Carry a phone with you at all times. Have special business cards printed up with your work number, home number, cell phone number, beeper number, voice mail number, e-mail address, your best friend's number, the super's number and the phone and fax numbers of your next-door neighbor who wears the thick stockings rolled down on her varicose-vein-covered calves. An answering machine should be connected to every phone. Yes, even your cell phone. Get a bigger purse.

Be available AT ALL TIMES. Don't EVER give him the excuse of not being able to reach you. If he is not available when you want him, threaten his pets. If he even thinks of doing it again, play the tape you made of Squirmy's torture session. Make him carry a beeper at all times. You are an adventuress. You need stalkable men the way a big-game hunter needs water buffalo.

If you really want a man to know you're interested (or simply want to get under his skin and make him regret that he ever dumped you, that son of a...), call him obsessively at all hours of the day and night.

Men have very short attention spans and can easily be diverted by ESPN, the wind, a ball of twine or even practicing their favorite yo-yo tricks. Let them know you're after them. This will make them nervous and easier to catch. Consider hiring a private detective so you know where they are at all times. Tell them you've stalked potential dates (and their families) before.

Show them pictures.

Show them the ransom note.

Show them the ransom.

They will be very afraid.

Another good reason to call men is that you might catch them breaking the rules with some hussy who isn't you (though she could be *related* to you). If they are out of breath when they answer the phone, pretend to believe their pathetic story about running down from the attic. After you hang up, get right in your car and go over there to see who he's playing with. If she is thin and weak-looking, give her a clip up 'side the head. It's always best to let a man know you mean business right from the start.

If you call him and he wants to get off the phone first, you may think he's not interested in you. It's time to pleasantly remind him who's boss. Make him want to stay on the phone. Tell him what you're wearing. Tell him what you're doing. Tell him he has five seconds before you set off the bomb in his office. Whatever you do, don't wallow in self-pity. Why should you be uncomfortable if he's not? Make him appreciate every minute in the sack by making the rest of his life a living hell.

Calling him incessantly will give him the impression that you are complex and interesting. It's always better when you call the man, especially if you reverse the charges and route the call through a South American long-distance service. That's because you are in control and prepared—you had a few shots of vodka and a pack of cigarettes. You're ready to sit back and let him in on the twisted workings of your brain. You have deep, significant questions ready for him, such as: "How pretty do you think I am, really?", "If you were trapped alone on a desert island with me, how happy would you be?" and "Do you still think I put sugar in your gas tank?"

Always leave an outgoing message on your machine that lets your dates know where you are and when you'll be back. It will prevent them from thinking they can make other plans because they don't know where you are. Call in for messages every 15 minutes so you can always capitalize on a dating opportunity. Women who break the rules can be ready at a moment's notice and never let a live one get away.

BTR women don't mind getting hurt. How many times have you found yourself writhing in agony as you crammed yourself full of Oreos and pork rinds trying to forget the humiliation of being thrown out of a married man's house stark naked? This kind of experience can't be begged, borrowed or bought. It has to be aggressively gone after, and BTR women know how to do it.

If he's in love with you, he won't mind if you call him compulsively. If he's not in love with you, who cares what he wants? Find out what time he goes to sleep and always call 35 minutes later. Wake him in the dead of night as often as possible. Lack of sleep will confuse him and make him an easier mark.

Don't be surprised if a man tries to wait as much as a day to call you after a first date. Put a stop to this kind of game-playing by telling him you've made an appointment with Dr. Kervorkian to help you end the searing pain he's causing you. Invoke his mother and all the pain he's caused *her* as often as you possibly can. Let him know about the pain *you* can cause her if he doesn't shape right up.

What if you want to call a man when you know he's asleep or busy? Feel free. Day or night. We have a friend who used to call her date before she went to bed and keep the receiver under her pillow with the connection open. Every time she woke up to go to the bathroom, she'd hold a bullhorn up to the phone and shriek, "Are you asleep honey?" The man soon moved in, just so he could get some sleep.

What if the guy can't take it and actually tries to leave you (or refuses to post bail)? WHY would you want him to stay? That slimeball. Let him go. But *never* return his stuff, especially if you've managed to pinch a credit card or two. Just work fast—you only have a short time 'til your rival, if she's a true BTR woman, makes him get *her* all new cards.

5

Gab until his ears bleed

In Rule 496 you learned the importance of calling a man at all hours, preferably when he's asleep. If, by some fluke, a man has worked up the courage and interest to call *you*, keep him on the phone for hours, at least two. We recommend one of those cute kitchen timers (we prefer the ones that allow up to 24 hours before dinging) that can go off after a good part of the morning or evening has been wasted on a senseless call.

Keep him on the phone by telling him everything you can about yourself. If he actually tries to do any talking himself, let him know in no uncertain terms that just because he's paying for the call doesn't give him the right to ruin a good rant. Make him listen to every chapter of your sordid past and wretched childhood, year by year, month by month, day by day.

Or start out by sharing what happened when you first woke up. Then discuss how breakfast, lunch, and dinner went, moving along to important topics like "My cactus is blooming," "I think I'm catching a cold" and "I've been hearing voices. They want me to hurt you."

Explain in vivid detail how you're sure someone is trying to sabotage you at work. Ask him over and over again what you should do. Ask him if he thinks you look fat. Ask him if he has a better formula for a pipe bomb than you do. Ask him if he thinks you look fat. Read him the latest research on cellulite. Ask him if he thinks you look fat. Bore him to tears! Then, after a few hours, when the lovely ping of your kitchen timer goes off, say sweetly, "Gee, this has been swell. Gotta run!"

Invest in an excellent long-distance carrier. Get the "Friends and Family" calling program and sign up your new boyfriend immediately. You could say something like, "I know we've just met, Stan, but I'm sure I'll be calling you a lot and we'll be talking for hours." He'll be stunned and agree out of fear for his life. Of course, using *his* calling card is even better, but that can wait for a week (but no longer!).

BTR women know it's better to talk on the phone than sit staring at the walls stuffing their faces with Cap'n Crunch. Another good advantage to incessantly talking on the phone is that you'll leave him exhausted and unable to talk to any other woman that might call. Tell him all about the trouble you had changing the kitty litter. Read aloud from *Waiting to Exhale*. He'll be too sleep-deprived to speak to anyone for days.

You may feel cruel keeping him on the phone until his ears bleed, but you're actually doing him a favor. When he finally sees you in person, he'll be thrilled and delighted. At least when he's with you, he knows you won't be calling him. And he'll take you places to shut you up. He may even try to keep you out all evening, taking you to place after place, based on some distorted, laughable theory that that will tire you out. Ha! Call him at the restaurant table from a pay phone.

Sometimes a man will try to trick you by turning off his answering machine. Just keep calling and letting it ring. When his machine reactivates, leave dozens of messages. Make sure at least a quarter contain some reference to cutting instruments or sensory deprivation tanks. There'll be no need to pull that stunt ever again. He will be trained (at which point you can bring up the dog collar idea).

You might lead some men to nervous breakdowns. That's okay. It's *good* when a man freaks out and starts to go insane. That's a sure sign he cares about you. When he's ready to change his number and move to Des Moines, calmly reassure him that you have a life. Tell him then that on many nights you will be out doing your own thing. Of course, you still expect him to let you know exactly where he'll be every minute. Some things are nonnegotiable.

6

If he has a pulse, you have a date

Saturday night is the night that you prove to yourself, society and the universe in general that you are attractive. So we don't care how you do it—just make sure you have a date.

Why would you turn down someone with a Gold Master-Card just because he called Saturday at 8 p.m. to ask what you're doing...at 8:30? Hey, a man's attention and credit line are nothing to sneeze at. If a man even accidentally dials your number (yes, wrong numbers can be fabulous sources of exciting dates), jump on it!

BTR women seize opportunities. The phone rings. It's that annoying telemarketer who has been trying to sell you the water filter system for your kitchen sink. Buy it if he agrees to install it on Saturday night. Insist on dinner beforehand. Choose the restaurant and eat as much as you can. Hell, it's Saturday night and he's picking up the check. It doesn't get any better than this. (Don't forget to return the filter bright and early Monday morning.)

Some women shy away from going out with nightmarishly ugly men with bad breath and sweat stains. Will he take you to the restaurant you can't afford? Does he have a platinum card? Is he breathing? Then why be so picky? (Of course, if he really is a dead ringer for Xythsckyll, the Peruvian God of Oozing Wounds and Solid Waste Disposal, put a bag over his head.)

Of course, *you* don't have to be pretty to break the rules. Plain girls with skin rashes and overbites can break the rules just as easily as blonde, ponytailed cheerleader types. You can be fat. You can have dirty hair and fingernails. You can wear spandex even though a tent would be more appropriate. You can wear pink sponge hair rollers. *Any* woman is free to break the rules. (And feel free to beat up those ponytailed cheerleaders.)

If you made plans with your girlfriends before you got that call for a date, by all means cancel them. They would dump you in a minute, too. If they are very good friends, don't cancel. Impress them by bringing your date with you on a jeweled lead. Berate him and fondle him alternately until he and your friends despise you.

Should you date bald men or, worse, bald men who wear toupees or, worse yet, those who have a single strand of hair growing somewhere in the middle of their back that they wind and wind and loop and curl all around their head, firmly believing that no one will notice? How should we know? Why are you asking us these questions? Do you expect us to answer these inane hypotheticals for free? More importantly, what do you do with a man who wears a *real* rug, some piece of carpet he just cut up and plopped on his head? See how insane these questions can become? Can you blame us for not answering any of them, since we know many of you will simply skip to the next page if we make this paragraph long enough?

7

Stupid things to do waiting for your date to arrive

It's easy to obsess about an upcoming date, especially if he's been stalking you. But it's healthy to spend the week before the date fantasizing about it in your mind, talking incessantly about it with your girlfriends and writing long, bitter diatribes to send to him if he doesn't like you. Preparation is the key.

Waste little time with unimportant things, like your job, eating, grooming and exercising. You want to compulsively build that dinner and movie into the mountain of your dreams, so that when it crumbles you will be fully prepared to wallow in the Trough of Despair. (You can tell we're incredibly cool, literate writers because we use capitals and stuff to make things Really Important. Damn, we really charged too little for this book. You would obviously have paid more for authors who KNOW HOW TO USE CAPITALS, wouldn't you? We really should rethink that line of Breaking the Rules fashions. Can we sell you a coffee mug? Wanna buy a T-shirt?)

If you've already composed your wedding announcement, picked out the bridesmaids' dresses, printed the invitations and finalized the menu with the caterer, here are a few really stupid things you can do to get yourself in the mood for that date to come:

1. Wrap your thighs in cellophane and stick them in the microwave. Maybe they'll shrink.

2. Sleep all day, then two hours before the date, get up and binge on an entire box of Twinkies.

3. Try on every piece of clothing in your closet. Squeeze and bleed your way into those size 6 jeans. Cry when the fat spills over the sides.

4. Belt down a six-pack of beer. See if you can do it in under five minutes.

5. At the very last minute, try your hair in different styles you've never tried before, from the French twist to the beehive. Minutes before the date, when it's too late to change it, settle on looking like Phyllis Diller for the evening.

6. Tattoo his phone number to your chest.

7. Call his mother and tell her the date to leave open for the wedding.

8. Go to an insipidly romantic movie that will leave you miserable over the fact that you'll never do the nasty with any of the Baldwin brothers.

9. Write your name over and over again the way it would look combined with the name of your favorite movie star: Jennie Pitt. Jennie T. Pitt. Mrs. Brad Pitt. Jennie Pitt. Jennie T. Pitt. Mrs. Brad Pitt.

10. Stock up on tons of contraceptive gel you'll never use.

11. Buy a feminine hygiene spray. Try it on the parakeet first.

12. Call Dionne Warwick at the Psychic Friends Network. Spend at least $200 asking for details about your upcoming date. Make sure you charge it to his calling card.

13. Get a pap smear.

14. Defrost your refrigerator.

15. Call him every five minutes and ask why he isn't there yet. Begin early on the morning of the date.

16. Repot your houseplants.

17. Repot your neighbor's houseplants.

18. Repot your neighbor's pot.

19. Repot your neighbor.

8

Make your first date last at least 48 hours

As you read this book, you might think *Breaking the Rules* is too risky and wonder, "What if I am so self-centered and self-absorbed that I end up alone for the rest of my life? What if the bookstore won't give me my money back for this cheap ripoff just because I've spilled ketchup on every other page? And what is the square root of 247 anyway?"

On a first date, your priority is to overwhelm him. Plant yourself on the steps of his apartment building on Friday morning so that he can see how much you are looking forward to your Saturday night date. When you see him for the first time, burst into tears and scream, "I love you, I love you, I love you!" Every few minutes, no matter where you are, lay down on the floor and offer yourself to him. If you are after a particularly elusive man, offer him money. Keep mentioning marriage—the marriage of ideas, the marriage of flour and water to make cake, The Marriage of Figaro. Let these casual mentions work their subliminal magic. Always carry several romantic Hallmark cards in your purse to whip out, sign and present to him at every possible opportunity.

Wear a Hawaiian muumuu to his office Christmas party. Come on to his boss. Do whatever you need to do to make sure he never forgets that you are a woman to be respected, a woman to be reckoned with, a woman to be feared.

Be up-front and honest about your neuroses. Let him know you're currently under a doctor's care and that you're hoping to reduce your antidepressant prescription from three to two pills a day.

Making a date last for days and days isn't easy if the man has a job or a home of his own. You must, however, do your best to make him block out a 48-hour time period. He might need to be coaxed a bit at first—ipecac in his morning coffee is a good way to make sure he dips into his sick leave for you.

If he says he has to get up early for an important business meeting, taunt him about being a workaholic geek who better change his ways if he ever wants to get any again. Tell him you're busy the next day, too. The fleet is in.

Never, never, *ever* end the date first, unless his ATM refuses to advance him more money. A BTR girl gives an impression of immense stamina. If he can stay out, so can you. If you are tired, take a nap. Many fine restaurants have rest rooms with comfortable chairs and sofas. These are perfect locations for during-the-date naps. He'll wait, because you've taken his wallet with you. If you carry a large enough purse, you can even bring a loose-fitting shirt to help you sleep more comfortably. Make sure to hang up your dress so that you will still look fresh and beautiful when you get back to the table several hours later.

Make it clear he has nothing to say about actually ending the date. You will go home when you are good and ready and not one day sooner. Glance at your watch after nine or ten hours and say, "Gee, this is just starting to get good."

If you are having an especially good time on the date, try to make it last forever. Dinner was good. The movie was good. Dancing was good. Why stop there? How about more drinks and a late-night snack? Worried about how your hair and makeup are holding up? Just grab a cab to the nearest hotel that advertises hourly rates. Most of these will have a least a few rooms available with mirrors placed over the beds. You can lay on your back and look at yourself until you think of somewhere else for him to take you. We shouldn't have to tell you to have his credit card handy before all such trips, should we?

Okay, okay, enough fun and games with elbow macaroni. How long should a first date *really* last? How long would it take you to memorize *War and Peace* in Turkish? Double it.

On the second date, make him move into an apartment closer to yours. Who wants a man more than seven minutes away when you call him in the middle of the night because your overhead light bulb burned out?

By the third date, it's time to bring in your lawyers and accountants for a complete analysis of your victim's, er, loved one's portfolio. The most important question, of course, is: "How much life insurance does he have?" In case something happens to the darling, you naturally want to be able to continue squandering money in the style to which you are becoming accustomed. The answer to this question, as any self-respecting life insurance salesperson will tell you, is, "Not nearly enough."

If you've been breaking the rules then you probably know that dating provides a fabulous opportunity to secure free housing. If you can get yourself into his apartment on the first date it is, in fact, possible to simply never leave. Cry. Scream. Hold onto the doorjambs. Yell "I'm carrying your baby, you monster!" when the neighbors check out the scene.

If you are intent, due to reasons of personal solvency, not to use him as a meal ticket, still make every attempt to keep him as insurance against a dateless Saturday night. If he doesn't ask you out again by the end of the date, refuse to get out of the car until he does. If he asks you out and you are not free that night, make sure you tell him in minute detail exactly what you will be doing instead, and with whom. He should know times, dates and your emotional position on everything...even if you have to make it all up.

If your lowlife ex left you with seven or eight mouths to feed, it's essential that you spring your urchins on your next unsuspecting male as soon as possible. The first date is certainly not too early—make him take the whole family to McDonald's! Then, over your Happy Meal, sob about how your ex never pays child support and how you're late on your house payments that month. As your kids fight over the fries, explain to him how there will never be a dull moment in his life if he agrees to support you and the kids. After the meal, ask him for some up-front money to buy some socks.

We have a friend, Gladys, who suffered through the pain of a divorce. She was then introduced to some guy named Hubert. On Gladys and Hubert's first date, she was candid about her ex-husband: "Even though Desmond was a nasty, vengeful, penny-pinching nightmare who broke my heart into a thousand little pieces, I'm not bitter. I still believe that by some freak accident of nature, there is one nice guy left in the universe. I am open to the possibility that *you* are that freak. I am willing to forget about that no-good, two-timing, lying, cheating, lame excuse for a man and get on with my life. Just don't expect much sex. I'm completely frigid."

Get to know his male friends. Call them up, introduce yourself and ask if their wives are available for baby-sitting. He'll love how quickly you took an interest in him and his buddies, and you'll have a bunch of new sitters.

Are the kids going to make dating tough? That depends. When you come home from a day's work at the auto plant and are late making dinner, do they come after you with a chainsaw screaming, "You're late again! Feed us now! Redrum. REDRUM!"

Do you frequently have to chastise them, saying something like, "Apologize, Jimmy, and promise the nice man you'll never bite him, choke him and set him on fire again."

How does your date react when you tell him your son Milton is in the basement, where he can just amuse himself for months at a time...as long as the neighborhood pets hold out?

When all else fails, convince your date that your 5-year-old son is almost grown and ready to move out. Say things like, "He's a fast learner, and I expect he'll be in college in a couple of years." Let him know you're ready, willing and able to send the kids to boarding school, hire a nanny or give them away to his Aunt Bruno.

9

Spill your guts before you spill your wine

Spill your guts. Go ahead, this is your chance! The primary purpose of dating is getting the opportunity to talk about yourself for hours and hours on end. This is also quite a money-saver since it eliminates therapy costs *and* comes with free dinner.

It's a great idea to break in a new man with your dating history. Tell him about the busboy you had to handcuff and beat up because he owed you money. This will give him a clear signal that if he uses your quarter to make a phone call, it is a loan, not a gift. Laugh with him about the time you went out with the seminary student who turned out to be a Lebanese transsexual. Give all your ex-dates cutesy names like Single Fat Father or Chins or Dingleberry.

If a man can be driven away, he should be. You only want the needy type who stay no matter what. These are the men who will take any abuse you heap on them and still buy you things. This will also save you money on personal assistants, maids and secretaries. A man who will pick up your dry cleaning and have sex on demand is worth keeping around, even if he does annoy you by breathing.

If you have beriberi or Lyme disease or rickets, if you suffer from dandruff, ingrown toenails or Munchausen's syndrome, this is the time to talk about it. Subject to chronic warts? What about those hammertoes and bunions? Confide in him about your difficult periods. Send him out for sanitary supplies so often that you can open up your own tampon table at the local flea market. Don't hold back. *You're* on a date. *He's* hoping to get lucky. Make no mistake about who's got the upper hand.

Men have to feel like you're in big trouble so they can rescue you. Men *like* to fix stuff. Cars, trucks, cabinets, rutabagas and women. Sniveling about the wretched quality of your life and acting convinced that he can save you is an excellent entrapment technique. (Do this even if you *have* no problems.) If you can't tell him lots of sordid stories, show him. Signs of your gloomy past should be all over your apartment: Al-Anon brochures, Overeaters Anonymous stickers on the fridge, sleeping pills and your shock treatment schedule for the week.

It's also important to show him your messy dark side from the beginning. Here's a handy checklist:

- Leave bras behind the bathroom door. Let him know you're a slob now. If you can't pick up after yourself, he'll never expect you to pick up after him.

- Open your mail in front of him, especially letters from mom and dad with support money inside.

- Display framed pictures of yourself caught in compromising positions with your last boyfriend. Build a collage that chronicles your last 10 boyfriends. Have circles and arrows, charts and graphs explaining your inevitable nervous breakdown.

- Show him your checkbook. Confess that your idea of balancing it involves running to the nearest ATM machine to see the balance that comes up on the screen. Tell him if he helps you balance your checkbook, you'll whistle like Lauren Bacall.

If you have trouble talking about these things, by all means get snookered. Shots of tequila work well for us. Keep no secrets and never EVER listen to him talk about his problems. If he wants to talk about himself, tell him to get a sex change and date a nice man.

10

Move your stuff into his apartment as quickly as possible

If you enjoy a man's company, or if you are preparing for a second date, move in as quickly as possible. Before the first date is really best, though anytime before the third is acceptable. Crowd his place with lots of girly goodies, from wind chimes to refrigerator magnets. Rent a truck, a moving van, a camel, a four-wheel-drive or a hot-air balloon and get a bunch of stuff over to his house ASAP!

Moving in can be done one of two ways: 1) fast and 2) really, really fast. We'll begin with the fast method and start by telling you one of those long-winded, pointless stories of somebody else's life you probably care nothing about.

A friend of a friend's sister's mother named Edy was looking to get married after a recent divorce. She was at that age (over 18) where she had decided she had very little time to waste. She got set up on a blind date with somebody named Moe. He was somebody's second cousin twice removed from Uncle Larry who lives in Virginia, Curly's side of the family.

When Moe came to pick her up, Edy's bags were packed and waiting in the next room. After a hearty hand-shake, she got Moe to transfer her luggage, boxes, lamps, Post-Its, tables, plates, pencil cups, cats and other smaller stuff into his car. The relationship was moving a bit fast for Moe's taste, but Edy stayed in the car with the windows rolled up until he finally agreed.

The second successful formula for moving in with a man takes a week. During this very extended period of time, you can really get to know him, but commando tactics are still necessary. That's because if a man is given time to think about living with you, it could take months! BTR women don't have that kind of time to waste.

Go to any handy army-surplus store and pick up the following:

1) One camouflage outfit	$39.95
2) One 8-ounce can of green grease paint	$ 4.35
3) Army boots	$34.00
4) Canteen	$ 2.99
5) Climbing rope	$ 1.99
6) Staple gun	$ 3.15
	$86.43

Take all this GI Joe stuff home and put it on. Find some twigs in the backyard and use the staple gun to attach them to an old hat. Cover your face with that green paint. Then go hide in your boyfriend's bushes and wait for him to leave for work the next morning. (You don't really need the canteen or the rope. It just looked cool to put in the list.)

When he leaves for work, break into his house and start spreading your stuff all over the place. Put all your clothes in the closet, claim a small area of the medicine cabinet, put your shoes under the bed, your diet pills in the kitchen drawer. Bag and burn the army outfit.

When he arrives home that night and you're in some cute teddy and the pot roast is cooking in the oven, he'll think you always lived there. If he asks, "Hey, how'd that toaster oven get here?", tell him an army recruitment officer was giving them out at the local mall. He'll never know the difference, and you'll live as happily as you could anywhere else.

11

How to end a dull date without committing a felony

If you break the rules consistently, you will grow to feel very comfortable with ditching one man and picking up another. Occasionally we meet women who, though very capable of breaking the rules, have difficulty extricating themselves from a dull dating experience. Here is a list of useful but sensitive escape lines:

- Your mother paid me to have dinner with you, and her check just bounced.

- You make me sick. I'm leaving.

- The check's yours, that cab is mine.

- Look at the time! I've got to vomit.

- Love me, love my chlamydia.

- It's after nine o'clock! Oh, no, I'm breaking parole.

- Oh my goodness, I seem to be having a baby.

- I'm having one of my spells (begin dancing wildly on the table).

- The building is on fire. Gotta run!

- Ever try anything kinky with sheep?

- I have to go home right now. I left my wart remover plugged in.

- The moon is full. I'm going broke on depilatories.

- Should I ask my husband to join us? He's right over there.

- I wish they didn't crawl so much (while slapping your head).

- I don't feel as bad as I did the last time I got alcohol poisoning.

- I hope it's still this good after we're married.

- I think my brother would love you. Can I give him your number?

- I'm eating for two now! (Smile brightly.)

- It's so annoying being a carrier.

- The moving van is waiting. What's your address?

- You know, you'd look really good with just one arm.

- My furlough's over at 10 p.m. and Big Bertha won't be happy if I'm late.

- I've got a late date with the hat-check girl. Call me next April?

- Do you have enough life insurance?

- I'm eating for five now! (Smile very brightly.)

12

Married men take you to nicer restaurants

We never fail to be surprised when one of our girlfriends complains about being attracted to "unavailable" men. Ladies, please! To a BTR woman, EVERY man is available. It's simply a matter of *timing*. Don't be dissuaded by some little gold band around his finger. Who cares as long as he has an American Express gold card to go with it? Gold's gold. Get him to take you shopping. Go out go to dinner. After you've been fed and fooled with, send him home. NOW he's unavailable!

The main reason to go out with a married man is for the money or the services. Try a plumber or an electrician.

Get some work done around the house. Remember: There should always be something in it for you.

Planning a party? Short on cash? Have no fear, date the butcher. Flash him. Serve steak. Call the baker. Compliment his buns. Get some.

Date your married gynecologist. He already knows you. He's not going to ask how you got the scar.

Is he divorced with two older kids? Maybe his daughter wears the same size you do. Encourage him to buy her new clothes. His son is in college? Get him to get you tickets for the Bowl game. Scalp 'em. It's money in your pocket.

Merchant marines are good, too, since they're out to sea for six months at a time. Date him the night before he leaves, and collect the gifts from every port when he comes back. Send him back out to sea after the appraisals are done.

Speeding ticket? *Au contraire!* It depends on what you wear. Low-cut blouses, high-cut skirts. Smile. Cross your legs. Go 80.

What all these men have in common is that some shortsighted women might actually term them "unavailable." In this context, all "unavailable" means is that he won't end up in your living room scratching himself through his boxer shorts and picking his ears with a knife. He's got the little woman at home to share that with.

He's not unavailable—he's just not a burden. The condition of the elastic band surrounding his underwear will never be a concern of yours. You know who's unavailable? *You* are, for family dinners and his repulsive friends. If he's sick, you're busy. If he's got problems, you're working late. Wants to talk? You're on the road.

Who wants a man who lives only for you and stares lovingly into your eyes, even when you're trying to sleep? That could really interfere with your dating.

13

Use threats and a concealed weapon to land your dream date

For some of us the question is not "What should I do on a first date?" but "How on earth can I get a date without paying an escort service?" Many women get bogged down if a dateable man doesn't present himself in an easy-to-catch fashion. These women are big quitters.

You are going to have to become a networking fool to meet bunches of boys. Tell everybody that you're looking to meet men. Tell fellow students, business associates, family, your manicurist, your therapist and the meter man. Consider a discreet announcement like: "I'M LOOKING TO MEET SOMEBODY. DOES ANYONE KNOW ANY CUTE GUYS? I'M WILLING TO SETTLE FOR JUST ABOUT ANYBODY. I'M NOT DISCRIMINATING. I HAVE NO CRITERIA

REGARDING AGE, EMPLOYMENT OR RELIGIOUS BACKGROUND. MY PHONE NUMBER IS 555-0655. THAT'S 555-0655."

Scream this at the top of your lungs in a very visible place every quarter-hour. You might get lucky. (Minimally, you will get arrested and perhaps get to go out for a donut and coffee with the cop.) Hit on everybody you can in any situation possible. Here are some suggestions:

As your dentist is filling a cavity, gaze lovingly into his eyes. In the sexiest voice possible, ask for the drool cup.

When the tennis instructor bends over to pick up his balls, pinch him in the rear.

Your handsome chiropractor has you in a compromising position on his table. Sit up unexpectedly, kick him in the head and, when he's down on the floor (which may require a *series* of kicks), roll on top of him and say, "I'm sorry, my leg went into spasm."

Go house-hunting, even if you can't afford a brick. Force the real estate agents to give up their lists of eligible men that are moving into the area.

If you are lucky enough to live in New York or some other large metropolitan area, the public transit system can be a real gold mine. Always ride during rush hour to make sure you land a date who has a job. Make eye contact briefly, then glance down. Do this three or four times, then, when you are very near your stop, walk up to him and say something like "I'm your boss's sister. Do what I tell you or you'll never work again." Get his business card, then get off at the next stop.

Do you travel often? Airports are great dating opportunities. Get a businessman. Tell him you know shorthand. Help him pad his expense account and accumulate frequent flyer miles. Point out that for him seduction can be a deduction! "Write me off. I don't care. Can I have a second entrée please?"

The grocery store is a great meat rack. Dress up, wear heels, think cleavage. Meet him, hook him, get him to buy you groceries all in the same night! Take him home. Make him cook for you. What could be better than that?

If your neighbor has a boyfriend, invite him over to fix something. Lure him into your bedroom by telling him the ceiling fixture is jammed. Throw yourself at him. Tell him you know what you really want him to fix. Tell him you'll see him next Saturday…or you'll tell his girlfriend where he was today. Desperate times, desperate measures. She'd do the same to you, honey.

If you are utterly desperate, there is no reason not to sink to placing a personal ad. Let's face it, advertising has worked for Procter & Gamble; you might as well see what it can do for you.

If you do decide to place a personal ad, by all means lie. He'll find out you're not "young, lithe, with a dancer's body" soon enough. With any luck, the force of your personality (combined with a concealed weapon) could still make the date a success.

14

Be at your best with PMS (needy, clingy and whiny)

Your boyfriend should not be allowed to make any decisions on his own. Look what happened when he was allowed to buy his own clothes! He expects to be led around by women because, deep down, he knows we're always right. So make a list—no later than the second date—about everything he needs to change, including, at the very least, his clothes, car, house, furniture, paintings, hobbies, job, height, weight, genetic structure, friends and, if possible, parents. Show him you're the sweet lovable creature you know you are—give him a week, then give him the heave-ho. If he can't accept a little constructive criticism from the future mother of his spawn, what's a girl to do?

Change him. Change every conceivable thing you can, from his clothes to his taste in music, from the hair on his head to the hair on his chinny chin chin. But change him.

Some men will not willingly cave in. They will fight you, call the police, have you committed. There is no alternative: Such men must be broken. Be ruthless.

Most guys really *expect* us to change them. Who's going to tell them how they feel if we don't? That's because men really don't *have* feelings, so there really is absolutely nothing to discuss. The closest men get to what we consider the center of our lives is watching sports together, during which they may well, openly and without shame, scream, curse, hurl empty beer cans at the screen and even (shudder) blatantly share their pseudo-feelings, usually about pizza toppings or burps or cleavage. Count your blessings if this describes your paramour. Many guys don't even use words to communicate. They merely grunt, pass gas or hit each other, depending on circumstances. (A surprising number of our guy friends agreed that grunting, passing gas and hitting each other, usually during a sporting event but not necessarily in that order, were about all that was needed to really "share" with other guys.)

Given most guys' incapability of doing more than grunting—what passes in Guydom for "sharing" and "feeling"—sometimes you have to reinterpret what they're saying to get at the deep, inner wellspring of what they really mean.

For example:

He Says: "Pass the broccoli."

He Really, Deeply Means: "My inner child is naked and quaking. Please hold and cherish me."

He Says: "Do we *have* to go see *First Wives' Club?*"

He Really Means: "Pass the broccoli."

He Says: "Hit the road. You've spent all my money, thrown away all my clothes and redecorated my apartment. What's your name again?"

He Really Means: "Hit the road, etc., etc."

Since men reserve all their so-called emotions for sporting events, you must scream and yell at guys. *It's what they're used to.* So get drunk and yell at your man. He'll bring those same raucous emotions home to the bedroom in no time. We find it very effective, as we reach the climax, to yell out the name of his favorite team. Something like: "Oh, yes, YES. Let's go Mets. LET'S GO METS!"

What if he wants to do something on his own? This, of course, isn't a problem for those of you wise enough to schedule the early lobotomy, as we suggested in rule 39. But if you refuse to break the rules on a consistent basis, you will have to put your foot down (the throat is a delicious target). Unless it's mowing your lawn, buying you a gift, taking out your garbage, buying you a gift, taking you out or, gosh, we almost forgot, buying you a gift—no way, Ricardo!

Force him to do everything with you. Be needy, whiny and clingy. This will be particularly easy once a month—you will know when those days are happening and so, by god, should he—but practice, practice, practice so it comes naturally 365 days a year. PMS is a gift given to women, biological permission, if you will, to torture, maim and paralyze men. Throw furniture, start fights, threaten him with a butter knife and drink Drambuie. Hey, *we can't help it!* What kind of geek would fault us for a little emotional twister once a month? Complain loudly and constantly about feeling neglected, hating his mother and why none of his cousins ever called after the family reunion. If he doesn't sympathize and take care of you, leave him.

Do not for an instant believe that he has any taste or that he has a clue about how hominids act. Tell him what to wear, where to be and at what time. Suggest how much money he should bring. Introduce him to your family as soon as possible. Buy his dogs some bones. Force stuff to happen.

It's important that you completely push yourself into his world. Don't let any corner of his life be a mystery to you. Steal his little black book and white-out all those other women's phone numbers. It's important to white-out EVERY number, including his physician's, friends' and all of his family's. (You never know who they might know and introduce to him.) Make sure his world completely collapses around yours. Give him just enough oxygen to live off of, but otherwise, leave him weak and unable to date others by sucking all the life out of him. You can do that with a constant PMS approach to life.

Here is a classic PMS controlling conversation we suggest you memorize and try at home:

HE: "Hi, honey, I'm home!"

YOU: "Shut the ____ up. I'd kill you just as soon look at you! I hate you, your mother, your brother, your dog and your goldfish. By the way, I killed your goldfish and your dog is next. ARE YOU LISTENING TO ME? ANSWER ME WHEN I'M SPEAKING TO YOU. ANSWER ME, look at me, look at me, do I have to do all the talking, you think my butt is big and fat, don't you, DON'T YOU?

HE: "Uuuuhhhh..."

YOU: "Oh, honey, I'm sorry, I'm sorry, I don't know what I'm saying, I love you so much, my little honey bear, baby love, sweet smudgy face, I love you I love you I love you, what did you bring home from the store, you forgot the Häagen-Dazs, HOW COULD YOU FORGET THE HÄAGEN-DAZS, I sent you specifically to get the Häagen-Dazs, you miserable excuse for a creep, I curse the day I ever met you, ARE YOU LISTENING TO ME, ARE YOU???"

You get the idea.

15

Taking advantage of him is just another way to say "I love me"

You can use men to do things for you that you'd never do for yourself. All you have to do is insist on it. They will walk out in the pouring rain and get the car and drive it around so you don't have to get wet. We don't know why they will do this, but they *will*.

Men will open doors. They will carry bags for you. Think of them as beasts of burden. Use them. Men love to be worked. Encourage yours by saying things like, "I'd feel so much sexier if the grass were mowed. I'd even, you know, do *that*." (Always remember, for a man, empty promises are great motivators.)

If a man is very good, you will probably discover he has been trained all his life. Believe it or not, there are thousands and thousands of men whose mothers actually told them that they should open doors for women. *No matter what.* This archaic approach to male-female relations can be capitalized on. Some men would open the door for you if the room they were fleeing was under mortar attack. He would get to that door even if he had to stagger to it on bloody stumps. Then he'd use that stump to *hold it open for you!* Perfect!

There are many other useful manners men have been taught. For instance, a well-trained man will stand up when a woman walks into the room. When he does, take his seat. He's up; he can find another.

Always give a man your car keys to pick your car up from the lot. Dating is just a different way to get valet parking.

He's picking up the check, of course. Did you know that food paid for by a man has no calories? Oh, yes. This is the time to try the shrimp appetizer and the lobster bisque and the rack of lamb. This is *not* the night to pass on the banana flambé. Hell, he's buying—get the chocolate mousse too. What you don't eat you can take home.

Every time a man leaves your house, make sure he takes out the garbage. It will make him feel like a lion running out into the night to leap on the back of a gazelle and wrest it struggling to its death. Taking out the garbage is just like that to a man, only in a Hefty bag. If you don't have any garbage, make some. It's important to establish this habit early and never let it be broken.

When you're sick it's even better to have a man around. Nothing like an indentured servant. "Get me my NyQuil...buy me a magazine...I want soup...my pillow's too lumpy." Get all your errands run. "I'm so sick and my dry cleaning is ready. I just don't know what to do." He'll get it. He has to. He's been trained. Even if you're not sick, just call up and pretend to be. Consider it a well-deserved mini vacation. No need to tip.

If you're dating several men during the holiday season, remember that Christmas is the time for giving, so give them your list. You certainly don't want them to duplicate gifts. Decide what you want to get from each man and then nag him mercilessly until he gets it for you. Heavy dating in December can set you up for an entire year!

16

Don't get mad, get really, *really* mad: Sell his power tools and pepper his underwear

Men love hammers, wrenches, drill bits, lawnmowers and train sets. We believe there is a genetic difference (we won't say *failing*) that draws men to metal objects that make unpleasant sounds. We know one man who was so obsessed with his saw collection that he completely forgot to buy his girlfriend Judith any gifts for MORE THAN A WEEK!

Women who break the rules don't settle for this. When Brad failed to put the toilet seat down for the 4,700th time, this month, Judith knew it was time to gently explain his failings to him in a cool, rational manner. She waited until he was out at Sears buying replacement blades for his hacksaw. Slipping into the basement, she used the table saw to cut his golf clubs in half, the saber saw to hack through his pool table, the jig saw to carve curlicues into his coffee table and the circular saw for the bed (which he wouldn't need because she certainly didn't plan to be giving him any).

This may have been a mild overreaction. It is not always necessary to destroy things to make your man toe the line. If your paramour of the hour is more involved with his machinery than you deem to be precisely normal, it is possible to kidnap his power tools and demand good, solid ransoms.

First, find a way to get into his garage when he isn't there. We recommend calling the police. Cry as you explain that your husband locked you out again. With luck, they'll let you in...and put out an APB on him. After they leave, head for his workshop. His favorite tools will be the ones sitting out, the ones he uses most often, the ones he's probably most attached to. Snap up his Snap Ons! This is your chance to Black and Deck him.

Once you have his best tools, get out there as fast as you can and hide them in a safe place. Call him. Take his best drill bit and smash it with a hammer. Send what's left of it to him in an envelope. Include a note saying, "If you ever want to see your plumb line again, take the most beautiful woman you know to dinner." Needless to say, if you see him out the next night with one of your girlfriends, don't get mad, get even. Make him pay through the nose to get his tools back. Make him pay *with* his nose. Use the drill bit—it will really, really hurt.

Recommended ransom: dinner dates, Broadway shows, trips to Club Med, back rubs and washing your venetian blinds.

17

Stay in your jammies and catch your man in cyberspace

With 15,000 new subscribers joining a service like America Online every day, the chances of meeting men in cyberspace (which is, we've been told by our computer geek friends, actually a moldy basement in Bayonne, New Jersey) are great. And men outnumber women ten to one online! So, pack up your cyberbags and hop aboard the information superhighway in BTR style.

Almost effortlessly, you'll find yourself meeting men with screen names like LoveArrow, LoveHandles, Slow-Hand and Testiclese. And those are the printable ones.

You'll be able to choose from Paul, John, Jack, Steve, Steve and Steve. (For some reason when we went online we kept running into guys named Steve.) One Steve called, but he didn't leave his screen name, so we couldn't call him back. Was it Steve4two, SexySteve4U or SteamyStevie?

Well, it doesn't really matter, because there's so many men online that if you lose one, there're always tons more. Fake ones, real ones, fantasy ones...and maybe...the *right* one! And the cool part is you can talk to them while sitting at home in your jammies, eating your curds and whey.

Here are some other things you don't have to worry about on a cyberdate:

- What you look like.

- What you smell like.

- Water weight.

- Nose hairs.

- Nosebleeds.

- Your big nose.

- His big nose.

- Your recurring Tourette's syndrome problem.

- Your spouse in the other room.

Are you ready to go online and meet guys and spend more time on the Internet than on sleeping? Okay, start typing!

Chat rooms are places where people gather to talk to each other "live." They're sort of like 900 party lines, only people pretend it's more hip because it's happening on the Internet.

Always talk to the man first. Don't let ButtercupBabe get to him. Let's say you're in a room called Romance Connection, you see some guy named Blkndickr and you notice you share the same hobbies (crocheting, buffalos, high-stakes water polo). You could type him the following instant message:

"I really like your profile and screen name. My phone number is 555-0000. Can I come over in about an hour? I could hop in my car and probably make it in 45 minutes. Oh, hi, by the way, my name is Jennifer. I live at 456 Grove Street, which is exit 15 off the I-35 turnpike. I live alone, and I never lock my doors. We could meet at my place first. Did you *really* just break out of prison?"

E-mail is like regular "snail mail," only it's electronic. E-mail sent to a man you are interested in should tell him your entire life story and explain how desperate you are to meet a man, *any* man, even him. Emphasize the fact that you're willing to relocate. Send him a flattering photo of yourself, unless that's an oxymoron, in which case send him a naked portrait of your best-looking (female) friend. Say it's you and deal with the fallout later. Tell him exactly where you live and how he can use the key that's under your back door mat to drop by at his convenience. Give out your first and last name and next-of-kin residences and phone numbers, just in case he wants to meet the entire family on his own.

To get the most out of the Internet, create hundreds of false identities and stay online for days at a time. You might even meet a few of your cyber-dreamboats in person and experience the pain, degradation and embarrassment of being seen in public with misfit geeks and eggheads.

In reality, of course, the numbers aren't as wonderful as that ten-to-one ratio we talked about earlier. Follow the bouncing ball as we do the math and discover how many men are available on the Internet *right now:*

Let's see, so 15,000 people join America Online a day. That's 105,000 new members a week. Two-thirds are men—74,235 potential lovers and husbands for women online. Half of them are married, which leaves 32,914 eligibles. Two-thirds of these guys aren't even shaving yet, which leaves 10,410. Half of them have a mother fixation, leaving 5,202.5. Finally, subtract men with bad breath, compulsive eating disorders and hunchbacks, Peter Pans, Casanovas, Jesus Freaks and talk show hosts.

That leaves—drumroll, please—one. Yes, your eyes aren't fully dilated. One. One guy for all of us. So you'd better hurry up, ladies, because PlesurePrfect and LoveMuffins are typing like mad right now!

18

Your BTR
astrological
forecast

When you are stalking, er, considering a new quarry, it's essential that you also consider what the stars say about your union. Is his Pluto in the House of the Rising Sun? Does Goofy know? Is his Sword of Dramamine conjuncting your Tunnel of Love? Do air and fire signs mix, or will you both explode like swamp gas? If every newspaper has a different astrology column, and there are 1,589 daily newspapers, how can they all be right? Should Laura have Luke's baby?

Worry no more, we are here to prove your celestial dreams can come true! So put on some music by a Greek goatherder, grab a cup of Celestial Seasonings' Tummy

Mint tea and boldly go where every lousy tabloid has gone before. Here's your personalized astrological forecast:

Aries: Your temperament is more suited for leading small armies into battle than one-on-one love, so consider a *ménage à many*. Dominance is your specialization, leather your color. Through the month of October, the emphasis is on dressing your man. Implore him to wear more summer colors, unless, of course, he's a winter or an autumn, in which case shoot him in the head. Schedule the trial for November, when Jupiter is retronomolous and Saturn is sitting on your face.

Best days for planting corn: Wednesdays and Thursdays.

Your lucky number: 5,666,792,095,607,209.

Taurus: You'll be crabby from 10 to 10:30 a.m. the entire month of August. That's when Mercury hides from Venus and you'll have to return all those god-awful pillows you bought for the bedroom. With Neptune licking your feet for the next two months, you'll be compelled to eat everything in sight. *Of course* you're not happy sexually with your mate. Who would be? It's time to demand that penal implant.

Best days to build an ant farm: rainy days and Mondays (unless they always get you down).

Your lucky season: hockey.

Gemini: In the year 2000, from April 10 to April 12, early in the morning, you'll find yourself particularly chatty. Not to say you aren't *always* chatty. Chatty, chatty, chatty. He'll never get a word in edgewise and the conversation will be so shallow and one-sided that even if he did have a chance to talk, he'll have nothing to say.

Best days for grazing sheep: Thursdays, from 3 to 3:30 a.m.

Best days for grazing shepherds: any day but Thursdays, from 3 to 3:30 a.m.

Cancer: Your keyword is *clingy*. Possessiveness comes naturally to you moon kids. When he's in the bathroom with the door closed for too long, cry and moan about how lonely you are. Tell him he can just as easily go to the bathroom with the door open so you can talk. Mondays and Fridays, alternate side of the street parking is enforced.

Best days for waxing your thighs: twice a day (you're just too darn hairy for a woman).

Leo: Keep it up through May, Ms. Leo, and make sure the conversation is all about you, you, you! Scream and yell for the compliments you know you deserve. Say stuff like, "Aren't I pretty? Do you like my new outfit? Do you want to see your kids alive again?" Good days for looking in the mirror and posing are Mondays, Tuesdays, Thursdays, Fridays, Saturdays, Sundays and, oh yeah, Wednesdays. The man of your dreams will hardly notice you're more in love with yourself than with him. Just make sure in those moments of ultimate pleasure that you shout out *his* name, not yours.

Best day for calling the Psychic Friends Network: March 23 in the year 2003 (hey, that's when they *told* us you'd call).

Virgo: Allow him no room for error—criticize everything he does, says, wears or thinks. You've got that wonderful inbred ability to cut someone down to pieces with just the cutest wrinkle of your nose. Pull pieces of lint off his jacket and correct his grammar.

Best day for being a witch: like there are days not to be?

Libra: We don't really have anything to say to you, so here's a fun word puzzle. If a man leaves his house at 6:43 a.m. by foot from Albuquerque to get to your house in Wisconsin by 8:37 p.m. three days later and there's a wind sheer of 25 knots per hour and he's carrying 20 pounds of something heavy, what time does he arrive at your house? And if he's late, do you call to see if he's coming or wait 10 days to check it out? Is the answer: a) 10:30 p.m., b) right around lunchtime or c) not at all? The correct answer is, of course, d) nose hairs.

Your lucky credit cards: his Platinum American Express, his...wait a minute, you mean there are men with *other* credit cards? Amazing. Who dates them?

Scorpio: You libidinous sex fiend. You probably met your current submissive male in the Dungeons Chat room on America Online. Keep working your black magic, woman, and leave him panting for breath when you're done...sometime next Thursday. Tell him how proud you are of your praying mantis impression, then bite off his head after sex.

Best days for drinking Liebfraumilch: in the mornings before work.

Sagittarius: You laugh like a hyena. Use it to your advantage: Get faster service in restaurants by making loud scenes. Wail at your date's jokes until he turns beet red and slides under the table. While he's down there, make him lick your feet.

Best days for yodeling: 1:10 p.m. on Wednesdays.

Capricorn: Work, work, work. That's all you're good for. No one could possibly be more dull than you, except maybe Virgo. Go to Frederick's of Hollywood and buy the Pamela Sue Anderson underwear collection. If you can't seem to get your mind off the office, try some interesting love techniques with the tip of a number-two pencil.

Best day to hold up a gas station: October 21.

Aquarius: When the moon is in the seventh house, and Jupiter is kind to cars (c'mon, you know the words!)

then peas will gyrate Janet, and doves will kill off Lars. This is the yawning of the Aging Aquariums, Raging Nosterniums, I'm serious! Delirious...Come on, now, EVERYBODY SING! Never mind.

My dear Aquarian feline, you are a freak of nature. Whoever marries you must enjoy a woman who has trouble matching her socks. You march to your own drummer, and you checked out and turned the lights off years ago. You live in a world inhabited by strange ideas about electromagnetic fields and psychic phenomena. Pretend to be normal.

Lucky animals: slugs, all invertebrates.

Pisces: Stop drinking.

Lucky ~~fruit~~ ~~vegetable~~ ~~fruit~~ ~~vegetable~~ ~~fruit~~ ~~vegetable~~ ~~fruit~~ ~~vegetable~~ thing: olive.

19

Celebrities who break the rules

When it comes to bending, spindling and downright mutilating behavioral rules, guidelines, even mild suggestions, there are some women who simply soar far above the rest of us. And, of course, there are others who wouldn't even think of doing anything that dear old great-grandma didn't consecrate on her deathbed. Some of these women are famous, which means we can watch them take a bite out of life, or just bite the big one, right on TV.

Here's our list of favorite and least favorite BTR celebrities:

Women who take big bites out of life

Catherine the Great: We didn't really have the time or inclination to actually do any research for this book, so we don't know much about this Russian Empress, except that she slept with her entire army. Now there's a coup. Oh, yes, and something about a horse.

BTR Lessons: Make them line up and stand at attention. Load up on army supplies and hay.

Whoopi Goldberg: She rose above the limitations of being a single parent living on food stamps to win an Oscar, do one-woman shows and co-host *Comic Relief*, making almost as much money as Oprah, another BTR Babe.

BTR Lesson: Be very talented and generous and name yourself after a funny sound.

Mrs. Roper from *Three's Company*: The upstairs neighbor of Suzanne Sommers, Joyce DeWitt and John Ritter, she's the horny old broad who was always demanding sex from her exhausted and disinterested husband. She revealed the true power of the fuzzy pink bedroom slipper.

BTR Lesson: Accessories matter.

Madonna: A BTR Hall of Fame Founding Member.

Miss Piggy: Never before has there been such a glamorous, confident pig. Miss Piggy, the Zsa Zsa Gabor of the animal kingdom, always openly and doggedly pursues Kermit. She's okay with her current weight. Accessorizing is her specialty.

BTR Lesson: Speak in a high-pitched squeaky voice and bat your lashes. Maybe your frog will turn into a prince.

Ellen DeGeneres: Bravo to Ellen for coming out of her dress and admitting she's Lebanese on national television. (Danny Thomas must have been an inspiration.) We love her style and the fact that she brought The Village People on her show, not that anyone should imply anything from that.

BTR Lesson: To boost ratings during Sweeps Week, come up with clever real-life issues/storylines for your sitcom.

Geraldine Ferraro: Any woman with the *cahones* to run for national political office deserves BTR brownie points. We hope she's making a lot of money on the lecture circuit.

BTR Lesson: DO NOT run for vice president with Walter Mondale.

Katherine Hepburn: The real BTR deal—she never married, wore men's clothes and salvaged a career on the skids by producing herself in *Philadelphia Story*. Falling in love with the married Spencer Tracy meant never having to worry about being tied down as a wife and mother.

BTR Lesson: Get cast in a movie opposite Spencer Tracy and fall madly in love with him. This will be difficult because he is dead. Good luck.

Tweety Bird: She never let Sylvester the Cat catch her, but she always enjoyed the chase.

BTR Lesson: GET BACK IN THE CAGE!

Marge Simpson: Marge is truly the head of the Simpson household, in a dysfunctional, passive-aggressive kind-of-way. She rules with an iron fist, a gravelly voice and a blue beehive. And no one is going to tell her to get a new 'do! She's a reminder that stuff happens, but everyone can survive in our Toon Town world.

BTR Lesson: Let somebody else draw the pictures and come up with a storyline. You don't exist anyway.

Hillary Clinton: She's played the political game to the hilt. When her husband got caught with Gennifer Flowers and Paula Jones, she didn't even flinch (though we suspect he did by the time she got through with him). She wrote a book about a village (*not* The Village People), changed her hairstyle and got on with her life. And we just reelected her! (Uh, him, him and her, her and him, her and he, whatever.)

BTR Lesson: Be smarter than your husband and have a good hairdresser.

Just About Every Female Rock Star: Tina Turner, Alanis Morissette, Desiree, Bonnie Raitt, Joni Mitchell, Gloria Estefan, Linda Ronstadt, Sheryl Crow, Annie Lennox, Roxette, Sinead O'Connor, et al—we love you all and want front-row seats to all concerts.

BTR Lesson: Make lots of money being wild, crazy and free, but don't tear up a picture of the Pope on *Saturday Night Live*. And say no to drugs.

Now let's look at some of the women who are simply clueless. Maybe they stayed out in the sun too long. Maybe they baked too many cookies in the microwave. Maybe they are cookies. Somehow, it all went wrong. In addition to all those listed below, please include every country-western singer in the world.

Women who just bite

Tonya Harding: She skated her way into our hearts with her fat thighs and tacky outfits. Then she hired some thug to bust up Nancy Kerrigan's knee. Blaming it all on her husband was a good BTR try, but it backfired. At the end, she couldn't even keep her laces tight.

BTR Lesson: Never hire a thug who can't tie his shoelaces, either.

Olive Oyl: Let's be honest: Ms. Oyl could have used a little meat on her bones. And she wasn't too bright. However, she did manage to keep two guys fighting over her for 50 years, even though she never figured out that Popeye was a weasel, Bluto a slob and Wimpy the man with the plan (and the chain of hamburger stands).

BTR Lesson: Eat spinach!

Tammy Faye Bakker: How can we heap even more misery on the most miserable anti-BTR woman on the planet?

BTR Lesson: Wear waterproof mascara.

The "Snapple Lady": What happened to her? Why is she no longer reading fan mail on TV and giving away carloads of Mango Madness? Did she switch brands? Did her bosses can her?

BTR Lesson: If you get a job starring in commercials for a major beverage company, learn from the Dunkin' Donuts guy—get a 30-year contract.

Mary Jo Buttafuocco: Here's a woman who stood by her man until the bitter end, rather than booting him out the door by *his* bitter end.

BTR Lesson: Before opening the door, ask, "Who is it?"

Leona Helmsley: So only the little people pay taxes, huh? Ms. Helmsley, may we introduce you to your new prison matron, Ms. Lovechunks?

20

Aunt Land'em's agony column

Dear Aunt Land'em,

My boyfriend says he loves me, but I end up feeling very insecure about the relationship anyway. Lots of times even after a wonderful sexy weekend he will take days to call me again. What should I do?

Phoneless in Phoenix

Dear Phoneless,

Don't be such a chump. Why are you taking that kind of abuse? Are you saying that you actually put out for this moron? Never let the man have the upper phone. Never give him your phone number—always take his. Your first gift to him should be a beeper, then a cell phone. Call him frequently—every 20 minutes or so is a good way to start.

If he stops answering the phone, hire a surveillance team. A good team would consist of a middle-aged divorced retiree from law enforcement, a large oldish car and a young overweight actress wannabe. The car should be grayish green with a switch cleverly controlling the headlights. When he rounds the corner, switch off the right headlight. Next corner, switch on the right, switch off the left. Next you have both on. He'll never notice!

If complete surveillance becomes difficult, hire a helicopter and SWAT team. The main thing to remember is: He is your man, and we don't care what it takes, don't let that sucker go!

Dear Aunt Land'em,

I always go on double dates with my twin sister Mindy and her boyfriend Bill. Well, I'm sure he means well, but Aunt Land'em, all of Bill's friends are dopey and nerdy, they wear white socks, they have bad breath, bad hairdos, and that's if they even have hair. What should I do?

Single in Seattle

Dear Single,

The solution should be obvious: Go on a diet, get plastic surgery, dye your hair, then steal your sister's boyfriend.

Dear Aunt Land'em,

My boyfriend is wonderful all year long, and then football season comes along and it's as if I don't have a boyfriend at all! What should I do?

Lonely in Louisiana

Dear Lonely,

Well, your first mistake was in letting him watch TV, let alone have access to the remote control. Keep him on a short leash, that's the best plan. If in spite of your supervision your man actually gets to see football, spend the next 12 months making him regret it. Tell everyone you know how you have never really recovered emotionally from the time he abandoned you for an entire evening just when you needed him the most. If this doesn't work, hire a professional boxer. Every time your boyfriend even glances at a football player, instruct the boxer to give him a good right hook, a stiff jab, then finish him off with a rabbit punch. By the time he wakes up, the game will be over and he'll have plenty of time for you.

Dear Aunt Land'em,

My husband stopped wearing his wedding band. He says he's gained weight and it no longer fits. Maybe this is true but it still hurts my feelings. What should I do?

Bandless in Baltimore

Dear Bandless,

Dump him! You don't need that overfed cheating liar. Place an ad in the personals: Single again, very attractive, sensual woman seeks man, ring size 8. If the ring doesn't fit the man, find the man to fit the ring.

Dear Aunt Land'em,

I love my husband, but after 17 years of marriage I just feel like I cannot pick up another sock. My husband leaves everything right where he drops it. I'm embarrassed when our friends and neighbors come over and find underwear hanging from the living room lamp. What should I do?

Maid in Madison

Dear Maid,

The best thing to do if your husband is an Oscar Madison type is to go out and have an affair with a Felix Unger. You can invite your paramour to your house when your husband is out of town on business. If he's really obsessive, he will not be able to relax and have sex with you until he has washed all the dishes, put all the clothes away and scrubbed and waxed all the floors.

Dear Aunt Land'em,

I bought this other book and have been following the rules they give without fail? I always wait for a man to talk to me first? And I never call him back? I hang up after two minutes on the phone? And we haven't had sex even though we've been engaged for six years? And I think he's gay? And I think I'm gay? And...

Questioning in Quebec

Dear Questioning,

What are you, 12? 'Cause only prepubescent girls would use question marks at the every sentence, know what I mean? Are you crazy? Do you think I really care? Will you please put yourself out of your misery before I have to come up there and do it for you?

Dear Aunt Land'em,

I've been living with my boyfriend for seven years and I love him, but I just don't know what to do. Everywhere we go, he stares at other women and makes comments about their bodies. It makes me feel so fat.

Lardbutt in Larchmont

Dear Lardbutt,

Shoot him.

21

Keep breaking the rules, even if the police try to stop you

Some women are surprised when their friends, neighbors and/or family members are a little disturbed about their breaking the rules. Some of this is justified. It is annoying to have to get up at 3 a.m. for the third time in a week to drive two towns away to post bail for you. On the other hand, this is simply the kind of support you expect from people who love you. Some people are just so selfish!

Your parents may try to get you to settle down, get a job, go through rehab. Don't listen to them. They undermined you for your whole childhood. Don't let them get the upper hand again. Whenever you visit, dye your hair a different color. If you don't want to pierce your nose, eyebrow or lip, you can buy little magnetized versions that look like the real thing. They are not particularly comfortable over a long period of time, but, let's face it, if you visit your mother and she really believes your nose is pierced, you aren't going to be staying very long, are you?

Break the Rules with your entire family at all times. If they start calling too often, for example, send trained tigers to attack while they are hanging out the laundry. If they insist on rehashing arguments from your childhood, get a good flow of hot lava going through their individual homes. (It is best, of course, if they are asleep at the time.)

If you haven't been a big drinker before this, now is the time to start. Just drink—anything, anytime, anywhere. A Tequila Sunrise is a great way to start the day. Carry around those minibottles of cheap vodka. If you see a handsome man, suck one back. We guarantee that after a few shots you will be breaking some rules, perhaps even some laws.

There are people who believe that complete emotional honesty is not socially acceptable. Bullpucky. Be yourself. If you're preparing for a date and discover that your favorite pants are now so small that Kate Moss couldn't get her *feet* into them, by all means explore this issue with your date. What could have caused this? Who is to blame? Surely you didn't gain weight from eating! You couldn't have. You don't really eat that much. Prove it. Treat him to a dramatic account of your menus for the past three days. Whenever possible, include exact portions.

You can use any situation in your daily life to practice breaking the rules. Be outspoken and rude everywhere. Start at work. The next time your boss asks you to place a call for him, demand to know if he has broken his dialing finger. If he thinks you should serve coffee at an important meeting even though your title is *not* Mesopotamian Slave-Girl, trip, fall, throw the coffee at him, then apologize by telling his clients that you are so sorry but you haven't slept in 72 hours since he makes you do all the work and then clean the whole office. Watch him squirm. If he tries to fire you, sue for sexual discrimination.

Set him up for a sexual harassment suit. Fall into his lap while a cohort gets a Polaroid. Explain to him what your new job title is. Enjoy his expression when you come in everyday at noon (your new starting time).

22

Beauty and diet tips for BTR babes

Getting fat isn't really something to aspire to, but let's face it, food tastes great. What's *really* the point of subsisting on rice cakes and Melba toast for the rest of your *crème brulée*-starved life? Not eating leaves you too weak to fend for yourself. Next thing you know, you'll be living off some guy who's got enough energy to get out of bed in the morning because *he actually eats stuff*.

So *don't* give up food for men. Many men may leave you, but both Ben *and* Jerry are always waiting for you in the freezer, ready to embrace you in their nutty, fudgy, pralined arms, day or night.

There's another good reason not to get too thin or too pretty: If you become a knockout, your love interest will quickly tailspin into the Well of Insecurity. He'll become convinced you've met someone else or that you could never settle for a slouch like him. About which, of course, he's completely right, since you couldn't really generate a lot of enthusiasm for his slug-like existence when you were life-boat-sized. Now that you've Jazzercised your way out of Cellulite City, why *would* you want to stay down on the farm?

And now on to a very important topic: exercising. In a word, why bother? Wherever you go to work out, some skinny-necked, butt-lifted, perky-breasted aerobics instructor will make you feel miserable about your pathetic body. You'll never be able to get the Stairmaster to blow smoke the way she can. And killing yourself in the latest Spinning classes and Power workouts only leaves you vulnerable to getting fat again. You take it off, you put it on. Take it off, put it on. Why not just keep on that extra five to 10 pounds permanently?

Many books have been written about dressing to catch a man—dressing for success, dressing for power, dressing for salads. Our inclination is quite simple: Wear whatever you darn well please. The stuff you really want to wear you can't fit into, so you might as well put on the comfy, stained stuff. Clothes with big holes—but strategically situated safety pins—are perfectly acceptable, as are the sweats and muumuus you wash once a month, without fail.

What about makeup, you ask? What do you mean you didn't ask? Who the heck is writing this book anyway? (I told you we charged too little for it. These people are ingrates. Oh, shut up and finish the paragraph. There are no real... No, no, get out of the damn parentheses first.) Ahem, there are no real tricks here. Let's face it, you'll never be Cindy Crawford anyway, so why waste the time and the money? Keep using the same old mascaras, foundations and lurid lip colors you've been slapping on for years. And *never* pay for one of those humiliating makeovers in department stores. Why would anyone sit in bad lighting, without any makeup, so some prissy, beehived saleslady can cluck and squint at "the problem areas" before saddling you with a $200 bill?

These are but a few of the secret beauty tips we plan to detail much more when we write our sequel, *Staying Out of Jail While Breaking the Rules*. We'd tell you more, but we just found out that we are *not* getting paid by the word, and that each chapter should be no more than 2,000 words or we're losing money on every word we write (1,998), so (1,999) we (2,000)

Breaking the Rules
at a glance

1. Force yourself on men and tell them what they're thinking

2. Stare straight at men and talk incessantly

3. Meet him anywhere and tell him where to go

4. Carry an answering machine in your purse

5. Gab until his ears bleed

6. If he has a pulse, you have a date

7. Stupid things to do waiting for your date to arrive

8. Make your first date last at least 48 hours

9. Spill your guts before you spill your wine

10. Move your stuff into his apartment as quickly as possible

11. How to end a dull date without committing a felony

12. Married men take you to nicer restaurants

13. Use threats and a concealed weapon to land your dream date

14. Be at your best with PMS (needy, clingy and whiny)

15. Taking advantage of him is just another way to say "I love me"

16. Don't get mad, get really, *really* mad: Sell his power tools and pepper his underwear

17. Stay in your jammies and catch your man in cyberspace

18. Your BTR astrological forecast

19. Celebrities who break the rules

20. Aunt Land'em's agony column

21. Keep breaking the rules, even if the police try to stop you

22. Beauty and diet tips for BTR babes

About the authors

Janette Barber is a professional writer and stand-up comic currently employed as a supervising writer for *The Rosie O'Donnell Show*. She has toured as a national headliner in major clubs across the country and is considered to be one of the funniest women on the circuit today.

Laura Banks, author of the just-published *Love Online* (Career Press, 1996), is a regular contributor to America Online and is heard weekly on the nationally syndicated radio show *Online Today* (Dick Clark's United Stations Radio). She is also a contributing writer/humorist and guest speaker with the Microsoft Network and Prodigy's Pseudo. She's been seen on CBS, CNBC, USA Network, The Sci-Fi Channel and Fox TV as an expert on cyberlove. Her column "Love Online" can be seen in *Single Living* magazine. Laura can be reached online at http:\\www.laurabanks.com.

Index

Breaking the Rules

Oprah, see Uma

Passing gas, see The Distillation of Methanol Using Bovine Emissions, men

Rolls Royce, 34

Saran wrap, underused fashion accessory, 1-24, 25-68, 69-127

Telephone, 2, 4, 6, 8, 10, 12 and all even-numbered pages

Telephone chats with girlfriends, 1, 3, 5, 7, 9 and all odd-numbered pages

The Village People

Thighmaster, see Suzanne Sommers

Those little tiny hairs that grow out of his nose and you just want to take a pair of tweezers and yank 'til he squeals like a pig and...oh, sorry, we're saving that for the sequel

Uma, see Oprah

Van de graf generators, and first date, 666

War and Peace, 344-790 (vol 1)